Zen DOG

Music & Massage
for a Stress-Free Pet

Zen DOG

Music & Massage

for a Stress-Free Pet

Janet Marlow

METRO BOOKS
NEW YORK

Book and package design by Suraiya Hossain
Illustrations by William Cypser
Dog photograph © Photodisc

Metro Books
122 Fifth Avenue
New York, NY 10011

ISBN-13: 978-1-4351-1037-3

Printed and bound in China

10 9 8 7 6 5 4 3 2 1

Dedications

To my husband, Alan Brennan, and our sons,
Colin and Ross
For our circle of family love

And a special dedication to "Rags,"
who enlightened me to the ways of a dog

Contents

Introduction

Musicians and dogs have a lot in common. They both understand the power of communicating with sound. They both use volume and pitch to express reactions to their environment. And they both understand the value of harmony for well-being.

I've been a performing musician all my life and I have had the pleasure of playing in front of audiences in concert halls and outdoor festivals, creating a bond—person to person—through music. For me, the few seconds between the time when the music stops and the audience begins to applaud are very special. These are the few moments when both the audience and I are in the "now"... as if we are all taking a breath together before the next moment of our lives begins. This, in fact, is the normal state of being for dogs. They live in a continuing present and it is their eagerness to engage us fully in this way that has endeared dogs to humans throughout the centuries.

Today, dog owners are in a new era of caregiving. We love our dogs and we want the best for them, so much so that we are not just caring for them but are actually helping them evolve as a species. Their world is no longer confined to our backyards or barns. They travel in cars; go for regular checkups at the veterinarian's office; go to the groomer for haircuts and baths. They go on vacation with us; they wait for us in our homes while we are at work. If we're lucky, we sometimes take them to work with us; and if they're lucky, we schedule play dates for them with other dogs and find them their own personal pet sitters. We love our dogs and treat them as members of our family.

The intensity of the daily human experience greatly affects canine senses. My research on canine hearing sensitivity comes from my desire to use the power of music to help your dog live a calm and harmonious life. Using music designed *specifically* for the canine hearing range is a natural way for dog owners to help their pets feel more relaxed and less stressed. Music can diminish separation anxiety, nervousness during thunderstorms and in veterinary environments, on car rides, and for the hours when they are home alone.

Therapeutic massage techniques for dogs also have health benefits and provide a wonderful opportunity for you to experience caring touch and bonding with your pet. The massage techniques seen in *The Pet Owner's Massage Guide for Dogs* DVD in this kit may increase relaxation, reduce pain from chronic conditions, maintain an optimum state of condition, and promote overall well-being.

Combining the massage techniques on the DVD with the *Relaxation Music for Dogs* CD should help your dog become calm, healthy, and, most of all, *very* happy!

—Janet Marlow,
composer and researcher

CHAPTER ONE

Calm Dog, Healthy Dog

Why do so many people

share their homes with dogs? As people delegate more and more of their daily tasks to technology, spending time with our canine friends provides a welcome connection to the world of nature—and to our own *human* nature.

Our dog's acute senses alert us to sounds, smells, and sights that we would not ordinarily tune in to. Dogs look to us to provide a trusting, loving family and to satisfy their need to connect.

Dogs have a remarkable ability to observe our behaviors and routines. Sharing our home with a dog is a wonderful, daily give-and-take of dog-to-human expressiveness. Isn't it always a joy when your dog excitedly greets you at the door, bursting with happiness because you've come home? Even if you've only been gone for fifteen minutes, the excitement upon seeing you is the same. This loyal connection brings a special vibrancy to our home environment.

Whether we live in the city or the suburbs, we can readily engage our dog's amazing sense of smell, sight, and hearing. However, establishing behavioral parameters in a non-natural environment as a dog grows can be a challenge. Dog behaviors based on stress, separation anxiety, or aggression can develop as reactions to the environment as perceived through their canine senses. Evaluating your dog's behavior in response to its environment is the key to finding solutions to problems.

In this book, I'll describe a broad approach using music and massage to help you understand the subtle things that influence your dog's behavior. I'll help you create an environment for supreme doggie well-being. Learning about your dog's hearing sensitivities is an enlightening pathway to understanding a major part of your dog's life. Using relaxation music as a tool for creating a calm and reassuring environment for your dog will achieve positive, repeatable results. Mastering canine massage techniques will help you enhance your dog's physical and mental health.

The *Relaxation Music for Dogs* CD, *The Pet Owner's Massage Guide for Dogs* DVD, and the chapters in this book are all tools that will help you give your dog the best life possible.

Why is a calm dog happier and healthier than an anxious animal? Evaluation of a dog's health and well-being has traditionally focused on the physical state. However, the environment that surrounds our dog—the air, the smells, the sounds, the emotional frequency of our home—is an important consideration when we weigh their needs and behaviors. In addition to taking care of the basics of shelter, food, and family, we need to be aware of the vast range of sensitivities, emotions, and behaviors that contribute to doggie wellness.

When we neglect the more subtle aspects of canine health, we and our dogs both suffer the consequences. Nervous dogs can express such severe separation anxiety that their owners feel forced to put them on medications to calm them. Aggressive dogs can become so agitated when they are left home alone that they frantically release nervous tension by chewing furniture. Providing your dog with an atmosphere of calm can resolve subtle reactive behaviors before they flair to a serious level. By focusing on your dog's environment—and how he or she reacts to the surroundings—you can improve your pet's mental and physical health.

It's important to realize that canine "calm" does not mean your dog is inactive or lying down. Webster's defines "calm" as: *not agitated, tranquil, steadiness under stress, peaceful, quiet.* When "calm" is used in relation to weather, it is defined as "an atmospheric condition without significant wind or rain." Looking at a dog's life from these two perspectives—what is their internal state and what is their environment doing to affect this state—provides a holistic method of evaluating canine behavior.

A dog's environment can have positive or negative influences on behavior. You don't have to look further than dog shelters to find examples of high levels of stress, nervousness, fear, and anxiety. We can assume that many of these dogs came from negative environments that created, or at least exacerbated, these conditions. With their loud barks and bodily shivers, they are calling out to us for safety. Thanks to these shelters and the good people who manage them, these animals have a temporary respite until a caring person or family brings them home. Shelters give us a vivid look at why animals need the feeling of connectedness and safety in their environments, whether provided by their own species or ours.

A Holistic Approach to Canine Wellness

We are fortunate to live in an era in which canine (and human!) health is no longer evaluated solely on the basis of biological factors. Many veterinary facilities are incorporating a much broader definition of animal healthcare by including natural health practitioners alongside their traditional veterinary practices and treatments. The same holistic methods that benefit humans—massage, acupuncture, aroma and aqua therapies, and organic diets—can also benefit our dogs. Today, you have many choices to help maintain your dog's health.

Understanding Their Doggie World

Your dog understands the world through his or her sense of smell, sight, sound, taste, and touch. Dogs that are free to roam outdoors have the freedom of unlimited movement in reaction to their environment. In our homes, a dog's senses and movements must adapt to the limits of the non-natural environment. There are many ways, though, that we can help them feel comfortable and confident within a home environment. Whether we live in a small city apartment or a spacious home complete with a sprawling backyard, awareness of our dog's acute senses is the first step toward making him or her feel confident, calm, and secure. Below I'll touch briefly on several factors that influence calm and confidence through balancing your dog's lifestyle, physicality, environment, and health. You'll learn additional practical solutions to common problems in subsequent chapters.

A SAFE HOME

For a dog, home is wherever *you* are. It can be with a family of one or ten. Your dog can relax and rest in your home because the environment and consistent routine feels safe. Dogs thrive in a home that reinforces feelings of connectedness and safety.

As a family member, a dog learns the smells, voices, and behaviors of everyone in the household "pack." Anyone who visits your home will also be filed and categorized in your dog's sensory memory. As your dog goes through investigative behaviors with visitors, remember that you and your guests are a different species and your dog is simply seeking safety and balance with foreign introductions into the environment. Creating a consistent, canine-supportive environment in your home will have a tremendous impact on how your dog interacts with humans and achieves a balance of instinctual and learned behavior.

HEARING

One of the most overlooked sources of canine behavior is their acute hearing ability. Does your dog run away from fireworks displays or hide under the bed during a thunderstorm? The hearing sensitivity of your dog is amazing—the range of frequencies that dogs can hear is almost twice that of humans. You can appreciate this acuteness when dogs hear sounds and alert you to them before you can perceive them yourself.

Understanding how environment affects our dog through its hearing is a new approach to understanding—and resolving—canine behavior issues. If we are sensitive to this acute canine ability, we can create environments that accommodate our dog's hearing sensitivity and elicit more relaxed, confident behavior in varying scenarios.

EXERCISE

Any trainer or pet sitter will tell you that a calm dog is a well-exercised dog. Going outdoors is an event that all dogs look forward to and need. It is an opportunity for them to activate all their senses: smell, sight, hearing, taste, and touch. Dogs are athletic by nature, and regular exercise will give your dog a welcome release from pent-up house energy.

Walking or running with your dog is a wonderful way to get exercise for yourself (See Chapter 5: Rhythms, Walks & Companionship for more information.) If your dog is on-leash, sharing your pace of walking or jogging and communication through the leash can be an important part of developing a mutually beneficial relationship. Off-leash outings require even deeper levels of trust. Incorporating regular exercise in our dog's life is essential to his or her well-being, whether our dog exercises with us, alone, with groups of people, with other dogs, or with other animals.

NUTRITION

"What is your dog eating?" is the first question to ask when someone talks about a problem his dog is having. When we bring a dog into our home, no matter what stage of his or her life, we need to educate ourselves about the best nutritional choices for its breed, size, and condition. Nutrition is a vast topic and requires discerning actions on the part of the dog owner. You have to be careful not to project human eating habits onto your dog. Meeting your dog's needs as a member of your family means learning the amount of food your dog requires, how many feeding times a day are most beneficial, and how many and what kind of treats are reasonable for your dog's diet. It is an ongoing process until you find the right formula for your dog's weight and balance of health at each stage of life. Always make sure there is clean water available. Of course, it is hard to prevent occasional instinctual scavenger eating behavior when your dog finds that special "something" on the road—or countertop—to eat. That's what I call doggie fast food!

HEALTHCARE

Even though your dog may prefer a run in the park over a visit to your veterinarian's office, checkups are an extremely important part of evaluating and maintaining your dog's health.

Animals as pets are an integral part of our lives. Doesn't your life come to an emotional standstill when your dog gets hurt or becomes seriously ill? And don't you feel tremendous relief when your veterinarian diagnoses the problem and provides the proper treatment? The abundance of veterinarian offices and animal hospitals around the country is evidence of our commitment to keeping our animal companions healthy and physically sound. This progress for our pets stems from many international research communities in the field of veterinary science that further the base of knowledge that helps our pets live healthier and longer lives.

REST TIME

Rest is a state that allows a dog to relax his alertness and take a break 0place to rest at home. Consistently stressful home environments will have a direct and negative impact on a dog's ability to rest, and affect behavior and health. Conversely, consciously creating an appropriately

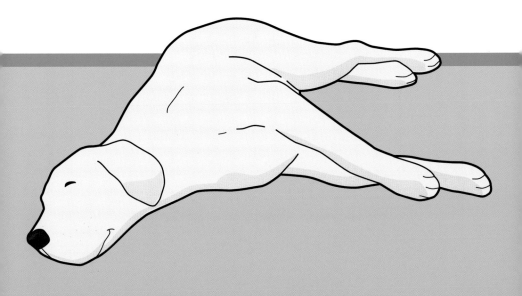

calm resting environment for your dog can solve many behavior problems and strengthen your human-canine connection. There are hundreds of choices in the marketplace for canine beds and other creature comforts. Accommodate your dog's nesting instinct by making a special place in your home for your dog to rest.

REACTING TO SOUND

Have you ever noticed that opening a window in your home changes the behavior of your dog? Or that your dog runs to the window howling at something you don't see? Your dog's acute sense of hearing plays a significant role in determining his or her behavior in your home.

Air is a conduit for the frequencies and volumes of sound that stimulate subtle behavioral reactions in dogs. For example, many dogs become stressed during a thunderstorm or find the whine of a vacuum cleaner agitating. Understanding the environment and the affect it has on your dog's acute hearing is a great tool for dog owners in evaluating behavior and resolving issues. (Read Chapter 2: The Magic of Music to learn more.)

ROUTINES

Dogs like routines. Routines help them synchronize their energy cycles. Dogs are like our personal built-in alarm clocks. Many dog owners notice that their dog wakes them up within a few minutes of the same time each and every morning. They bark or nuzzle us when it is time to get up in the morning and make it clear to us when it's time for a walk or to let them out in the backyard. They let us know when it is time for their meals and when it's time to go to sleep for the night. Dogs instinctually follow their internal signals for routine to keep their daily lives in balance. A dog's routine reminds us that we, too, should balance rest, play, eating, and sleeping in our daily lives. There are *so* many reasons why it's good for us to live with dogs!

ADVENTURES

Adventures happen when you and your dog find new places to explore together. It can be as simple as a walk to a different part of the neighborhood, or as invigorating as a hike along a nature trail. Whether your dog is on or off leash, discovering a new place can be a stimulating experience that breaks up expectation of the usual walk. Every new encounter is an opportunity to communicate and strengthen your bond, whether you take your dog into a place of business, let someone stop to pet your dog on the street, or simply take a moment to appreciate your surroundings together. Most often, we lead our dogs where we want to go. But it can also be fun to let your dog take the lead while you try to follow what he or she is sensing. No matter where you live, you and your dog can share the excitement of a new place together.

SOCIALIZATION

The goal of canine socialization is for your dog to be able to engage in social behavior with people and other dogs while remaining calm and receptive to your commands. Have you ever had an excited, muddy dog jump up on you *before* the dog owner was able to say, "Down! No jumping!"?

Dogs learn good socializing behavior through the assuredness and tone of your voice. Because dogs have acute hearing abilities, there is no need to yell your commands. Your dog should be able to focus on your spoken commands. The energy and intention you project in the *tone* of your command should be enough to communicate your wishes.

You and your dog need to practice socialization often. Visiting friends with other dogs or just walking down a city street provides hundreds of doggie socialization opportunities.

Today, well-socialized dogs can sometimes join us in our workplaces, visit the elderly at nursing homes, participate in dog therapy programs at hospitals, and even visit our children's classrooms. But just being with our dogs and teaching them to interact with our shared world is a creative aspect of dog ownership that will enhance your dog's ability to feel confident in any surrounding.

> *The goal of canine socialization is for your dog to be able to engage in social behavior with people and other dogs while remaining calm and receptive to your commands.*

Talking to Your Dog

Do you naturally speak to your dog in a higher register than your normal speaking voice? You are correct to do so! Dogs hear a much broader range of pitches than do humans, and they hear you best if you speak to them in a slightly higher than normal voice. (See Chapter 4: Beyond the Bark for more information.)

Dogs quickly learn to recognize the vocal qualities of their owners. I can call a friend's dog to "sit" with only random success while my friend can call her dog to "sit" with immediate, consistent results. Dogs react to our personal inflection and quality of voice in addition to the verbal content of our training commands. In addition, dogs also depend on pitch, volume, and emotional energy to understand our communications. We generally use higher pitches for affection and lower pitches for commands or reprimands. It is never just the words we say, but also the intensity and tone of what we are saying that our dogs understand.

Dogs, too, use a vast range of sounds for communication. Barking is only one of the ways they talk to us. Most dogs have about a four-octave range of vocal sounds (forty-eight notes), some of which are at the edge of the human hearing range. Listen carefully and you will be amazed by your dog's huge variety of vocal communications. If you mimic his or her pitches, you can have wonderful conversations with your dog!

NON-VERBAL COMMUNICATION

Dogs are like barometers, a gauge for subtle changes in their environment, because they remain alert to change as a survival instinct. They communicate to their own species in non-verbal ways, as when herds of animals move together to escape danger. When you become their family, they use these subtle communications with you as well. When dogs bark and wag their tails, it is easy to interpret their meaning. But there are many other ways dogs communicate through body movement, eye contact, and soft vocalizations. Professional dog trainers are especially adept at interpreting these movements and sounds. You can learn this, too, by paying attention to the natural behavior of your own dog.

Our dogs are aware of energy changes in the environment, even while resting. If you make a sudden move out of your chair, your dog will leap up and go wherever you are going, even if it is only to the next room. Your dog will sense your energy and match the tempo and mood of your movement. In the same way, you can experience your dog's subtle communications by matching his or her energy with eye contact, body language, and vocal tones.

BODY ENERGY

Dogs always want to make sure that you are not going anywhere without them. Accompanying you is one of their jobs. They enjoy being with you, whether resting by your side or checking out everything you are doing.

Non-verbal communication is a pure exchange of energy between you and your dog. Non-verbal exchanges are a great way to express kindness and love. Rest your hand gently on your dog and let it remain in one spot until you feel the warmth of energy emanating from your hand and being received by your dog. This is a wonderful way to soothe and calm your dog. He or she will immediately understand that you are offering a loving touch.

> *By focusing on your dog's environment—and how he reacts to the surroundings—you can improve your pet's mental and physical health.*

EYE CONTACT

Dogs speak to us with their eyes. When we lock eyes with our dog, we tap into his or her inner communication and energy. This is best with your own dog, as another dog may interpret this exchange as a threat. Gazing softly into your dog's eyes communicates trust and safety. Blink slowly while looking into your dog's eyes and in a short time you will get the same response from your dog. Perhaps this is an animal way of saying, "Yes, I love you, too!"

In addition to barks, dogs also communicate in vocal tones. If you want to have a good "conversation" with your dog, vocalize the same pitch that your dog is expressing to you, even if it is just a bark. Keep matching the tones as he or she vocalizes. Some breeds tend to do this more naturally than others. Engaging in your dog's language is a method of communication that can add some fun to your relationship.

Treats

Dogs clearly show us that treats are just about at the top of the list when it comes to best moments in a dog's daily life. We know that with a treat in our hand, we can train our dogs to roll over or give a paw or sit before us. As your dog matures, try taking this a step further. Instead of telling your dog what behavior you want in exchange for a treat, *ask* "What can you do for this treat?" Then wait for your dog to pick a trick to do for the treat. It may take some time for your dog to get it, but he or she will in time. He may offer a paw, or lie down or smile. She may make eye contact or lick or nuzzle you. Look for the most subtle body language and reward the action. It will be a treat for *you* to see your dog initiate responsive behavior.

Manage Your Dog's Environment

Our dog's reaction to the environment through his or her senses is our insight into the canine world. We become better dog owners by observing and acknowledging these most subtle reactions and behaviors. Engaging your dog with fun and creative ways of relating will support his or her lifetime doggie wellness. Establishing balance for the canine environment is a gift we give to our dogs, who give us so much every day.

CHAPTER TWO

The Magic of Music

Music is everywhere in our daily lives.

Music plays in our offices, in stores where we shop, in elevators, on our cell phones, and in medical and dental offices. Sometimes obvious to us and sometimes not, music is broadcast in these environments to evoke certain unconscious and involuntary responses to heighten our overall experience.

Studies have shown that music played in different environments will influence our behavior. Have you noticed, for example, that you may shop longer in stores playing pleasant music? And have you wondered why busy restaurants select upbeat music? They're trying to speed up the customer turnover. Music is purposely used in social environments to effect humans in subtle ways.

Music is powerful; it can change your mood and the feel of an environment. This is true for dogs, too. Dogs have extremely acute hearing. Low and high pitches and loud volumes can cause stress and anxiety for your pet. The good news, however, is that the power of music can also calm and soothe your dog *if* it's modified for his or her canine hearing sensitivities. And as a caregiver, you can use music to help address many behaviors and create the best possible life for your dog.

Doesn't it amaze you when your dog runs to the window barking and you look out to see nothing there? Yet your dog is telling you something *is* out there. After smell and sight, hearing is the next keenest sense dogs rely upon for survival in nature. In our homes, where they are limited in their movement, dogs can develop stress, anxiety, and aggression in reaction to sounds. I know of a dog that jumps into the bathtub to hide during thunderstorms. I have heard stories of dogs that ran away from fireworks events. Hearing is a sense that dogs use to help them adjust to cohabitating with us and that can result in positive or negative behaviors. Don't you often turn the volume down on the radio or TV if it's too loud? If dogs could make such adjustments to everyday sounds, would they? Yes! Understanding how your dog's hearing affects his or her behavior, and why and how music can play an important role in daily life, will help you become a better dog owner and give your dog a healthier, happier life.

When we bring an adopted dog or a new puppy into our home, his or her nose quickly learns our smell and the scent of the new environment. He or she learns to identify the furniture, which floors are slippery, and, most important, where the food bowl is located. Sound and your dog's hearing are important aspects of helping him or her feel safe at home.

Our dogs often make us aware of sounds that we can't hear. Observing your dog's reaction to different noises can help you identify subtle sources that influence behavior. For example, when the furnace is rumbling in the basement, your dog is not only feeling the vibration but is hearing the low frequencies that are not apparent to us. Your dog runs from the vacuum cleaner because the high frequency whirl of the machine is piercing to his or her ears. Acute canine hearing is an important part of your dog's life. Dogs can react to a sound within .006 of a second and hear up to four times the distance of humans. As you start to catch the moments when your dog reacts to sound, you will better understand your dog's life from his or her perspective.

Sound triggers your dog's fight or flight instinct, as you probably have observed many times when a door slams, a delivery truck drives past, or thunder rumbles overhead. On the other hand, sound can also trigger instincts of tranquility and relaxed behavior. You may have observed your dog resting on a patch of grass, soothed by the surrounding sounds of nature or curled up near you when your favorite music is playing. What you may not realize is your dog does not have the same audio/spatial localization ability that you have. Vibrations and jarring sounds in the music are indistinguishable from a loud vehicle or thunder. This uncertainty, combined with the fact that dogs cannot locate the source of these vibrations, causes them to react with defensive instincts. Sounds transmitted through the air that surrounds your dog are the most subtle and overlooked causes of reactive behavior. To better understand how sound can have positive *and* negative effects on your dog, it is helpful to understand just what sound is.

Your Dog and Sound

The air around us is filled with sonic activity—volumes of sounds, frequencies, and pulsating electro-magnetic waves. When sounds interrupt something we are doing or thinking, we react accordingly. For example, imagine the loud rumbling of a truck as it passes by. You can't see the truck, but you can hear and feel it. You mentally calm yourself by saying, "That was just a truck and I am not in danger." Dogs can only identify natural sound sources in our world, and therefore react to manmade noises by barking, running away from the sound, or becoming anxious. My dog Rags has heard our son practice drums in the basement many times, but on hearing that first drum roll, he immediately seeks higher ground at the opposite end of the house. A flee response is triggered by the strong vibrations transmitted through the floor.

Have you wondered how your dog knows to alert you *before* there is a knock on your door? Often, even before a sound, there is an accompanying sense that stimulates a dog's alertness. We don't know for sure how this occurs, but we have witnessed animals fleeing from impending earthquakes and tsunamis, perhaps expressing a "sixth sense." As dog owners, we have a special relationship with our pets in this regard. We share a delightful sensory co-dependency with our canine friends. We often rely on our dog's instincts to alert us, and our dogs look to us to communicate to them whether an event is "okay" or not. I believe this is one of the most heart-warming aspects of living with dogs.

Dogs can only identify natural sound sources in our world, and therefore react to manmade noises by barking, running away from the sound, or becoming anxious.

Sound can be measured in several ways, each of which helps us understand what can be agitating or soothing to our dogs. Alexander Graham Bell developed a measurement of volume, which we call a decibel (dB). Pitch or frequency—a "high" note vs. a "low" note—is measured in Hertz (Hz), named after the German physicist Heinrich Rudolf Hertz. We can understand the canine hearing range using these measurements and can compare them to our own range of hearing.

The frequency range of human hearing—depending on a person's age and overall exposure to loud sounds—is 20Hz to 20,000Hz. (The low E string on an acoustic guitar is measured at 82Hz.) Dogs—depending on breed and age—hear a frequency range of approximately 60Hz to 45,000Hz.

You can see by these numbers that dogs hear much, much higher sounds than we do. We intuitively know that they hear us best in higher tones. Don't you usually get the best reaction from your dog when you speak using a higher pitch than your normal speaking voice?

Another reason why dogs hear "better" than humans is that their ears have more movement, which maximizes their hearing potential. The shape of a dog's ear also helps it hear more proficiently. Upright curved ears help capture sound. If you cup your hands to your ears, you will enhance your own hearing. Some dogs' ears, like shepherd breeds, are naturally in that position. Hound breeds have acute hearing, but their floppy ears actually also help intensify their scent detection. Not all breeds hear equally well; frequency response varies with the size of the species' head, plus ear size and placement. The shape and placement of ears on different breeds are part of how nature has defined their role as a dog.

Frequency, or pitch, is only part of the issue. Volume also has a part in this equation. The volume range humans detect is 10dB to 150dB. For example, a soft whisper is 10dB, a normal conversation is 60dB, and the level of a loud rock concert is 115dB. Explosions reach 150dB.

According to the research of H.E. Heffner and R.S. Heffner at the University of Toledo Laboratory of Animal Comparative Hearing, dogs have a comfort level range of 60dB to 80dB (volume). This explains why dogs can understand your communications within the dB level of normal human conversation. When I consult with dog owners, I have them repeat their dog's name very softly to see at what volume the dog will perk up and look in response This is a good indicator of the hearing range of your own dog. Generally, low to moderate volume and non-jarring sounds provide the most comfortable atmosphere for dogs. (See Chapter 4: Beyond the Bark for more on frequencies of communication and dog language.)

Calming Your Dog with Music

Music is a language that your dog understands. It contains all the elements of sound that dogs use to determine the safety of their world. Dogs are discerning though. They will stay near sources of music that have frequencies within their hearing range and move away from music that is upsetting or extends outside their hearing capabilities. In the home, we should make sure to turn off the subwoofer or turn down the excess bass of a sound system—especially when listening to loud music with dogs nearby. Consider that a dog will "hear" ambient music approximately twice as loud—or more—than we do.

Using music to benefit animals in their environment is not a new concept. It has been documented that dairy cows produce more milk when listening to relaxing music; researchers believe that farmers could

get an extra pint from their charges by playing them classical music. Psychologist Dr. Adrian North and researcher Liam MacKenzie at the University of Leicester, United Kingdom, played music of different tempos to herds of Friesian cattle. Beethoven's Pastoral Symphony resulted in greater milk production. When loud and rowdy music was played, there was no increase in milk yield. North and MacKenzie hypothesized that calming music probably improved milk yield.

Your Voice

Dogs depend on the sound and inflection of your voice to understand what you want them to do. Have you noticed that when you are being affectionate, you instinctively talk to your dog in a higher-pitched voice? The higher pitch literally keys into your dog's natural (and higher)  frequency range of hearing. Your dog hears you better if you are speaking in a higher register, and higher pitches are considered "friendly." When you are expressing a reprimand, don't you instinctively lower your voice? The intention of your inflection is heard and understood by your dog.

> High frequency—"He's so cute!"
> Low frequency—"Stop! Wait!"

Pay attention to your vocal inflection when you're asking your dog to learn a new behavior. If you want your dog to stop jumping up on the person standing at the door, don't say "Don't jump!" in a soft singsong voice. Guess what your dog will do?! Instead, make sure your intention is clearly understood by using body language and a decisive command, like, "Down! No jumping!" Dogs need to hear the energy and intention in your voice.

Here is an easy experiment to try with your dog. Speak in different and extreme pitches, rather than the natural speaking voice that your pet normally hears and knows you by. Observe how your dog responds. Your dog may tilt its head, bewildered that you are changing your pet owner behavior! This is an easy way to see how animals respond to or "understand" our commands through pitch and hearing sensitivity.

Music for the Benefit of Your Dog

Now that you realize that your pet's hearing abilities are amazing, the next step is to learn how to use this knowledge to improve his or her behavior with controlled sound. The best-controlled sound we can offer is the sonic field of music.

AT HOME ALONE

Dog owners often leave the TV, radio, or sound system on while they are away from home. These are good instincts on the part of dog owners, who realize that dogs need the company of sound to make them feel safe and connected with their environment. Separation anxiety is the most common problem with dogs left home alone. When we leave our dogs at home, they feel our absence. They may howl and whimper, bark at the door, chew up furniture, scratch windows and sills, and have other destructive behavior. There is much good advice in books and other media about how to train dogs to control these sorts of issues. My research shows that music has many positive behavioral affects while dogs are home alone. When you use the *Relaxation Music for Dogs* CD in

> *Separation anxiety is the most common problem with dogs left home alone. When we leave our dogs at home, they feel our absence.*

this kit—designed specifically for dogs—you will return home to find your dog happy to see you because he or she has felt relaxed and safe instead of experiencing a day of separation anxiety.

Relaxation Music for Dogs was recorded for your dog's comfort. I have made the music dog-specific by eliminating the ultra-high frequencies (Hz) and the sub to low frequencies in my compositions. The titles of the tracks on the CD describe how your dog will react by listening: calm, deep rest, relaxation. Since we know that high and low frequencies have agitating affects, the elimination of these frequencies in the music allows your dog to be relaxed where alertive reactions would normally take place. The music on the CD is also compressed, meaning there are no sudden or dynamic changes in volume (dB). All of this comes together in the music for your dog's well-being. Play the CD any time you leave your home.

How to Use the CD

For best results, set up the *Relaxation Music for Dogs* CD contained in this kit in this way:

• Play the music at a moderate volume on your computer, CD player, or sound system.

• Position the speakers, CD player, or sound source at approximately ear level or slightly above your dog's head so he or she can feel and hear the vibration of the music. If your speakers are on the wall, know that sound is reflective and it may not necessarily be felt and heard by your dog if the music is playing far above his or her ears.

• Put the player on "repeat" so that the CD plays continuously until you return home.

• Start playing the CD for your dog a few minutes before you go out the door.

• Train your dog to associate the music with a "time to rest" command that you use before you leave the house.

When I leave my own music on for my dog Rags, I have trained myself not to emit an emotional energy along with the goodbye. I tell him to "protect the house," which is his job (every dog needs a job), and say "time to rest." Part of separation anxiety is the owner pulling on the dog emotionally and this energy is confusing. It's good to give them "loving limits." Dogs appreciate clear direction and

> *In the home, we should make sure to turn off the subwoofer or turn down the excess bass of a sound system— especially when listening to loud music with dogs nearby.*

they like to know their place. The music is soothing to them and they will rest the day away until you come home. Remember to pay attention to your intention when you want your dog to understand what you need him or her to do.

WHILE TRAVELING IN THE CAR

Regardless of breed, some dogs just love to feel the wind in their snout and the movement of the car. Other dogs display agitated and nervous behavior in cars, most likely due to the unsteadiness of the movement and the frequencies and vibrations of the engine. Some may be reacting to a negative association from a past experience. Engine frequencies and vibrations are very potent to some dogs' ears, and if we can help them relax just a little in the car, it is certainly worth the effort. Playing the *Relaxation Music for Dogs* CD can help mask common travel noises.

Travel Tips

Here are ways to help your dog become less anxious in the car so he or she becomes a willing traveler:

• Accommodate your dog's need to feel secure with a crate or a pad he or she likes.

• Take off your dog's leash in the car. The leash can snag on something and cause an injury. Your dog may also get confused and think he or she is going for a walk.

• Start the music in the car while it's still parked and wait a few minutes until your dog settles down.

• Give your dog a treat as a reward for settling down.

• Play the music in the car a little louder than in your home environment to mask the noise of the engine and street sounds.

• Stay calm yourself to help your dog overcome his or her anxiety. Dogs reflect our own behavior, which can escalate their feelings of anxiousness.

• Dogs do a lot of surfboard-like riding, gripping with their paws as they sway with our driving. Be aware of this when you are taking sharp and fast turns.

• Practice this sequence until you can see a difference in your dog's car behavior.

IN VETERINARY AND POST-SURGERY ENVIRONMENTS

This is a subject very close to my heart. It was while visiting a veterinary hospital that I was inspired to compose music to soothe and heal animals.

Veterinary hospitals have become very dog friendly, and adding relaxing music to the veterinary experience is an easy tool to help our dogs feel more at ease. Despite friendly human voices of welcome, a dog's first wave of experience once the door is opened is a potent perfume of many, many dogs and other animals. No wonder he or she shows nervousness about what's going to happen! Using soothing music to calm dogs is a natural fit for veterinary check-ups. Many dog owners who use *Relaxation Music for Dogs* at home have brought the CD to the attention of their veterinarians for animal hospital and kennel environments. Relaxing music broadcast in these situations will appease anxiety and provide a soothing environment for check-up rooms, overnight stays, post-surgery recuperation, kennel areas, and waiting areas. This music is also especially beneficial for dogs recovering from surgery at home. Owners of dogs with cancer or serious injuries have reported that the music allows their dogs to relax into a deeper state of rest during difficult stages of healing.

FOR PUPPY TRAINING

Music can be a gentle method of introducing your puppy to crate training and quiet time. When you are leaving home and it's time for your puppy to go into his or her crate (or during the night when it is quiet time), use the CD in the following manner:

- Place a portable CD player near your puppy's crate or nesting area.

- Play the music at a low to moderate volume.

- Put the CD on "repeat."

In time, your puppy will associate the pleasant music with settling down, calm, and rest.

DURING THUNDERSTORMS

The sound of a thunderstorm can reach volumes up to 110–115dB. The sound of thunder is disturbing to humans, so you can understand why a dog's acute hearing—combined with its sensitivity to atmospheric changes—can trigger behaviors of anxiety. There are some behavioral theories that suggest pet owners desensitize their pets to this experience by playing recordings of thunderstorms. I prefer the gentle approach of masking the sounds with music and have seen the success of these trials. If your pet is simply too anxious to handle the ongoing thunderclaps, use the CD to both mask the sound of the storm and provide an alternate atmosphere of calming music.

Bring the CD player to where your pet finds comfort, even if he or she is hiding under the bed. Play the music at a slightly louder volume than you would normally in order to fill the area with music. If you know that a thunderstorm is approaching, put the music on to settle the feeling of the environment in advance of the storm. I have heard from many dog owners about their dog's extreme nervousness during thunderstorms,

especially in regions of the country where thunderstorms are frequent and severe. Your dog's need to find a hiding place is instinctual, yet he or she has the physical limitations set forth in your home. In my consulting, I often hear the nervousness of the owner who is telling me about his or her dog's anxiousness. When using music and attempting to calm your pet, make sure that you are not projecting your own nervous energy back onto your dog. That energy will cycle back and forth. "My dog is nervous . . . I am nervous that my dog is nervous" and so on. Dogs are our teachers as they reflect our own energy back to us. Try the music and repeat the process during passing thunderstorms until you see diminished anxiety in your dog. You may find that the music calms you as well!

DURING FIREWORKS DISPLAYS

People often use fireworks to enhance a celebration. Fireworks used to be seen only in town parks and large venues, where there was a great distance between a dog and the sound source. Today, fireworks are readily available and are often used in the backyard of a nearby home. Imagine hearing the sound of fireworks and not being able to run far away to find shelter from the noise. It is quite common to hear stories of dogs running away from fireworks and being lost for days. Your dog feels and hears these sonic cracks with great intensity. If you do have fireworks occurring near your dog, be sensitive to this environment by:

- keeping your dog indoors.

- using the *Relaxation Music for Dogs* CD if your dog is staying in a room with the door closed.

- checking in with your dog after the fireworks are over and spending time comforting or massaging your dog.

FOR HOME GROOMING

I think dogs love to be groomed as much as we like the process of a professional hair appointment. We are giving them our full attention, which they like best of all. We are talking to them, touching them, and giving them the stimulation of water, brushing, and a final drying with a towel. They may just want to use the shake method while they run around to air dry. But if you use a hair dryer, listen for the high frequencies being emitted. Remember that these frequencies can be painful to a dog's hearing and therefore it is best to hold the hair dryer at a distance from your dog's ears. Be sensitive to your dog's reactions to the high frequencies of the hair dryer while you are asking him or her to stay. The *Relaxation Music for Dogs* CD creates a perfect ambience for home grooming. It will establish a calm atmosphere while your grooming turns your dog into a beautiful or handsome pet ready for a dog show . . . or just for parading in the backyard!

FOR REDUCING STRESS

You wouldn't think that a dog has stress. Some people would laugh at the thought. But when you start to become aware of their sensory experiences—as we have been doing by understanding their acute hearing abilities—we can begin to understand that all living creatures react to their surroundings. A few years ago, my friend's son used my *Relaxation Music* CD for a school science experiment. He had two potted plants and for a few hours each day he would play very loud rock music in front of one plant and my music for dogs in front of the other. Yes, you guessed it! The plant blasted with loud rock music withered while the other plant flourished. Every living thing is sensitive to its environment and we are becoming more aware of that fact.

Music and massage (see Chapter 3: Massage for Dogs) are great tools you can use to connect with your dog while addressing many issues, including stress. When dogs enter new environments, they rely upon their senses to evaluate their chances of survival. To them, survival means they are safe and can continue being a dog. Relaxing music is useful to create a calming atmosphere when:

- bringing an adopted dog home from a shelter

- introducing a dog to the family or another dog

- introducing dogs to your cats.

ADOPTED DOGS

I have learned from observing animals that meeting another animal is an evaluation process. Dogs don't waste any time determining if they are glad or not glad to meet another animal. Allow the newly introduced dog time to go through the checklist of its senses and begin to settle the stress of being in a new environment. Adopted dogs often have negative histories and the stress of entering a completely unfamiliar home is high. As you allow your dog time and space to explore and learn, you can get to know his or her personality as well. The background music will keep the atmosphere calmer for the excited family, especially when children take part. You will have to listen to your instincts to determine when massage can be introduced. Adopted dogs may have been physically abused, and the bond of touch may require a slow introduction. In time though, your dog may be nudging you for many belly rubs and massage sessions. Between music and massage, your newly adopted dog can have a healthy and happy life and will give you back that happiness tenfold.

MUSIC FOR DOG MASSAGE

If you have had a professional massage yourself, you know that massage therapists often use background music. The frequencies, vibrations, melodies, and rhythms of the music fill the room and become part of a calming environment that is meant to relax you. This is exactly what music does for dogs during a massage session.

Dogs will release tense muscle tissue as you go through the massage techniques you are learning from *The Pet Owner's Massage Guide for Dogs* DVD in this kit. The massage sequence will promote health, flexibility, and balance of movement and create a special bond with your dog through your caring touch.

DOGS AT THE OFFICE

Thanks to loving dog owners and company presidents who love dogs themselves, we have progressed in many corners of the business world to allow our dogs to come to the office with us. Whether at a home office or corporate office, our dogs can lower our stress, sharpen our focus, lower blood pressure, and keep smiles on our faces. It has the same effect on our dogs, as they don't have to feel separation from the person they love. Playing the *Relaxation Music for Dogs* CD in your office will help keep you and your dog calm until it's time to go for a walk. Don't be surprised, though, if your coworkers borrow the music for themselves or if your office space becomes the most popular to visit!

Good for Pet Owners, Too!

There is a secondary benefit to playing calming music for your dog. The music on this CD has been compressed and altered for dog listening and provides an extra calming influence on *your* environment as well. Our daily lives are often rushed, immersed in technology, and overly busy. Balancing this with calming music is good for the whole house. Taking a little time to be with your dog and listening to relaxing music is a good time-out from the day and is a gift to your dog of your company and your love.

CHAPTER THREE

Massage
for
Dogs

Touch is an important

part of every dog's life. Dogs let us know with their eyes, barks, and nose nudges when they need touch for comfort, assurance, and when they want to engage our attention. Just as clearly, we tell our dogs our feelings of affection through touch. It is a silent expression that transcends verbal language.

As humans, we know how caring touch is important for soothing the body. This has the same value for dogs. If you have been to a massage therapist, you know that the sequence and techniques of the massage session are methods developed to promote health of the human body and a sense of balance and well-being.

The *Pet Owner's Massage Guide for Dogs* DVD in this kit has been produced for you to learn through easy step-by-step instruction the basic techniques of canine massage to promote health for your dog. The techniques have been developed by the Bancroft School of Massage Therapy as a sequence of hand motions to administer to your dog safely and effectively.

Massaging your dog brings balance to your dog's physical life while creating a special emotional bond between the two of you. You probably give your dog the touch of massage just by the nature of your daily interactions, but it is good to take those hand motions a step further into a methodical sequence. It is also a good opportunity for you to do a body check of your dog—for example, discovering ticks, finding evidence of lumps, or identifying grooming needs.

You can use these techniques knowing that your dog can benefit by deepening his or her relaxation, preventing muscle injury, and by giving the gift of your company through the loving touch of massage. Your dog will benefit from massage because it promotes caring touch and bonding, increases calm and rejuvenation, reduces pain and chronic conditions, enhances athletic performance, helps in preventing injuries, increases comfort levels in geriatric animals, aids the muscular-skeletal system in maintaining good physical condition, and promotes overall well-being.

Sometimes when observing other dogs on the street, you can see stiffness in their walk or imbalance of muscles in their body. Even the simplest massage can decrease stiffness, soreness, and pain. Dogs' neck muscles react to a lot of leash pulling here and there and massage can release some of that specific muscle tension. Massaging your dog can diminish stress and nervous behavior. Applying massage to an older dog can increase circulation, flexibility, and range of motion. It's win/win for you and your dog!

> *Massage is also an opportunity for early detection of physical abnormalities and builds trust, especially if you have a newly adopted dog.*

Massage is also an opportunity for early detection of physical abnormalities and builds trust, especially if you have a newly adopted dog. Overall, massage enhances the health of your dog. If you are approaching a dog that you don't know and intend to apply massage, always keep yourself in a safe position. Never put your face in the face of an animal whose behavior you can't predict.

If this is a first time for your dog, the massage session might be cut short by your dog getting up and leaving the mat. Just let your dog go and, in time, he or she will understand the experience and you will be able to complete the full massage sequence.

It's Good for You, Too!

Massage is a wonderful way for you to relax and release your own stress, while taking time to sit with your dog. Give yourself a half-hour, turn off the cell phone, put on the *Relaxation Music for Dogs* CD, and begin to calm the environment and space for you and your dog for the session.

Setting Up the Massage Session

- Choose a quiet area to place a blanket or mat on the floor.

- Start to play the *Relaxation Music for Dogs* CD to bring a feeling of calm to the room.

- Relax yourself by taking three or four deep breaths while resting a hand gently on your dog's body.

- Let your dog choose a comfortable position. If this is the first session, he or she may not lie down or may walk away. That's okay. Gently beckon your dog to return to the mat.

- Be comfortable. Massage requires that you manipulate your body around the pet, so try to be aware of your own posture. This not only preserves your body muscles, but also helps to ensure that your technique is rhythmic.

- Keep your hands and arms relaxed to reduce tension that might be carried through to your dog. If you feel tension in your hands, stop and shake them out. It's all about fun, bonding, and relaxing!

Basic Elements of Massage Stroke

There are a variety of massage strokes you'll learn and each serves a different purpose:

Rhythm: as in rocking a baby to sleep

Contour: making your hands mold to the body part

Pressure: start with a very light pressure, about as much as you would use to brush your hair

Flow: make slow transitions from one body part to another

Sensitivity: try the stroke and pressure on yourself and then remember that your dog is much more sensitive than you are

Intuition and Communication: let your dog guide you as to how long to massage one area

Why French Massage Terms?

Many people know of Swedish massage therapy, which is the most commonly offered and best-known type of massage. According to *Massage Magazine*, "the Dutch practitioner Johan Georg Mezger (1838–1909) is generally credited as the man who adopted the French names to denote the basic strokes under which he systemized massage as we know it today, as Swedish or classic massage. Somehow, the term Swedish massage interchanged with the term Physical Movement System attributed to Swedish physiologist Peter Henry Ling (1776–1837). The term was transposed to Swedish Massage System sometime during the second half of the nineteenth century." Slightly confusing, but I believe it is always good to start out defining the origin of a subject when learning a new skill.

Things to Remember

- Don't give your dog a massage if he or she has any acute conditions, fever or inflammation, disk disease or rupture, wounds, or skin irritations.

- Remember to focus the techniques on the soft tissue.

- Avoid heavy pressure on bony areas.

- Start by doing each stroke in each body area for a count of six. After you have worked with your dog for a few sessions, you will find that he or she may like you to work in some areas longer than others. You can tailor your sessions to fit your pet's preferences.

- Always keep one hand on your dog. If you remove both hands, your dog will think that the session is over and may leave the mat.

- Use your intuition. If your dog doesn't like his or her paws touched and pulls away, then you should stay away from the paws. Same thing with the ears. Sometimes dogs' ears are very sensitive. If your dog doesn't like it, then skip that part. You want massage sessions to be relaxing and happy for both of you!

Learning
the
Strokes

The following are descriptions of techniques that have been developed by the Bancroft School of Massage Therapy™ (*The Pet Owner's Massage Guide for Dogs* DVD) as a sequence of hand motions to administer to your dog safely and effectively. Each easy-to-learn stroke will soon become a library of knowledge that you can use anytime your dog needs the focus of your skilled touch.

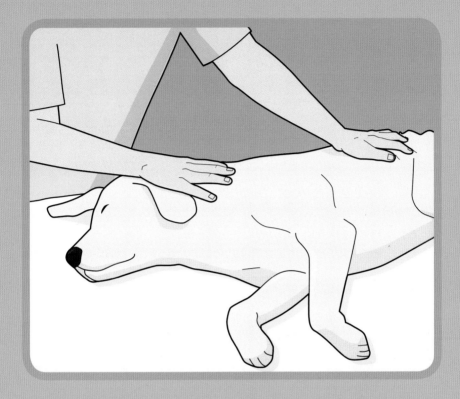

Compression

Compression is a technique that involves using the palm of the hand, pressing directly into the muscle and soft tissue of your dog's body. This stroke is done by pressing downward using soft hands with palms down, or by gently squeezing (compressing) a limb with your hands. Count 1... 2... then release and repeat until you have dealt with each body part and limb. After the compression, pause for a moment to feel the warm energy being emitted between your hand and your dog's body. This feeling is the massage working. As your dog will be laying on one side on the mat, find a gentle way to move your dog to his or her other side to complete the full body using the compression technique.

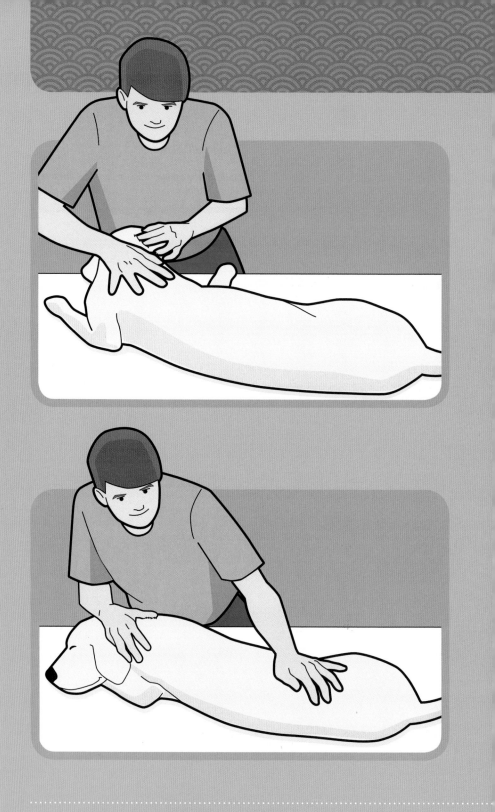

Effleurage

Effleurage, the French word meaning "to skim" or "to touch lightly on," is a series of massage strokes to warm up the muscles of your dog. The main benefits are in relaxing your dog and warming up the tissue to get the body ready for deeper strokes.

Using a gliding stroke, follow the flow and direction of your dog's fur. Make the strokes long, covering the whole body part. You can use your palms or fingers in a slow rhythmic motion, being careful not to press on bony prominences. On smaller dogs, use the sides or pads of the thumbs, instead of the palm, in long strokes. It is helpful to count to yourself slowly, repeating 1... 2... 3... 1... 2... 3... as you move down the body from the head to the torso. It is a good way to keep focused on your hand movement for this stroke, plus your dog will love hearing your calm breathy voice.

Effleurage is a good basic massage hand motion for your dog because it addresses your dog's full body in one stroke. The long, slow, and even-pressured movement can be of benefit to your dog, especially if you can only devote a limited time to a massage session and you are utilizing just the effleurage stroke. The *Relaxation Music for Dogs* CD is a good match to this stroke because the music contains long phrases and long tones, which work well with this hand massage motion. A few minutes of the effleurage stroke with the enhancement of the music playing may be all that is needed to give your dog a quick adjustment of energy, balance, and calming.

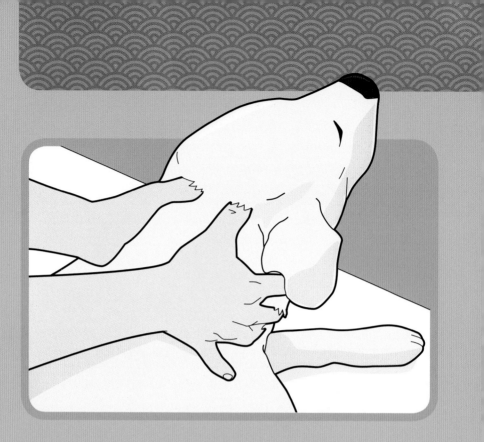

Petrissage

Petrissage, meaning kneading, is a semicircular stroke applied to the muscular areas of your dog. Here you use the palms of the hands on the larger muscles and the fingertips on the smaller areas. Use your fingertips for smaller dogs. Start from the head and work your way to the tail, finding larger muscles to work out those running and walking tensions. The web of the hand between the thumb and forefinger can also be used on narrow areas, such as limbs and the back of the neck. Making a shape like a "V" with your hand, practice using the web technique on your own arm first to understand how your dog feels the kneading and pressure. Web petrissage is good for the backs of the legs, along the front side of the hind legs, and down the backs of the hind legs.

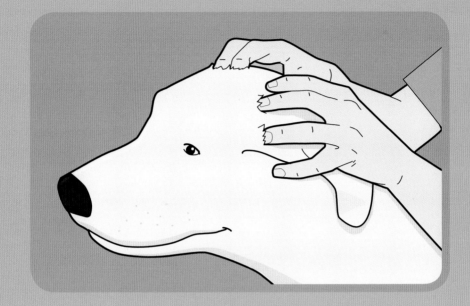

Vibration

Vibration techniques are made with a clawed hand position. Make an open claw shape with your fingers and thumb. Place it on a fleshy part of your dog, like his or her neck or shoulders, and shake and vibrate. Vibration can be effective by staying in one small area or by traveling to stimulate the whole body circulation. Vibration is good for loosening up tightness in the shoulders or the hips. Dogs really like this fun technique—and your complete attention, of course!

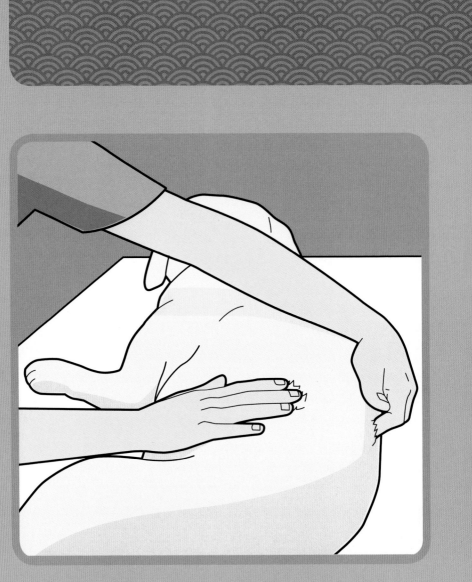

Rocking

This technique uses the hands to gently "rock" the entire body or limb. Use both hands on either side of the body or limb to gently create a wave-like motion. Move up and down your dog's body and he or she will completely relax, succumbing to your hand motions. Rocking is a finishing stroke to help sustain relaxation. Watch your dog melt into heaven with this stroke! So far in this chapter, you have learned the massage strokes of compression, pressing directly into

the muscle; effleurage, a long gliding stroke; petrissage, semi-circular strokes; vibration, vigorous motion; and rocking, gentle back and forth movement. You can begin to understand and observe that your touch, in these specific hand motions, stimulates physical responses from your dog. Just by using these hand motions, you can calm and balance your dog's energy level through massage. This is the power of touch.

Three Suggested Massage Sequences

As you practice and become more comfortable with each massage technique, you'll want to vary your sessions. Here are three suggested massage sequences: beginner, intermediate, and advanced. Mix and match techniques to mesh with your dog's personal preferences.

Beginner Massage Sequence

After you have a sense of the massage techniques from viewing the *Pet Owner's Massage Guide for Dogs* DVD, choose one of the strokes for a beginning session with your dog. Practice, for example, just the stroke of *compression*, which is as easy as gently pressing and releasing your hand all over your dog's body. Then at the next massage session, practice *effleurage* and so on. Each new session, pick one stroke until you know that you have mastered that technique. Do use the *Relaxation Music for Dogs* CD to enhance relaxation. This music is created just for your dog's listening comfort. In time, you will know the five basic strokes: *compression*, *effleurage*, *petrissage*, *vibration*, and *rocking*. Your happy dog will love all the attention no matter which stroke you use.

Intermediate Massage Sequence

Now that you have become familiar with the terms and what each hand movement does, you can begin to alternate two or three strokes as you and your dog become comfortable working together on the mat. Start combining two or three strokes. For example, use the long strokes of *effleurage* and then switch to *vibration* and then back to *effleurage* and then perhaps end with *rocking*. Mix the choices of two or three strokes each massage session to vary the learning sequence.

1. **Effleurage:** palm or the fingertips in the direction of the fur. Stay away from the spine. Use anywhere, i.e., along the rib cage, along the spine, etc.

2. **Vibration:** use in small areas or large strokes all over the body. Make a claw with your hand. Good for loosening up tightness in the shoulders and hips. If your dog is very tense, use large vibration motions down the whole body.

3. **Effleurage:** same long strokes following the direction of your dog's fur.

4. **Rocking:** finishes the session when your dog is quiet and relaxed. Create a neutral motion, moving back and forth. It is not a push and a pull. Gentle rocking increases your dog's relaxation.

Advanced Massage Sequence

Now that you have practiced and learned the full massage sequence, you have come to know your dog's sensitivities and your own intuition as to what your dog likes and what he or she dog doesn't like. Trusting these instincts is a silent communication between you and your dog. The full massage sequence techniques are tools for you to evaluate your dog's physical state and to enhance his or her well-being. Try to be a fair witness to the process and don't judge the technical flow. When it comes to biology, there is always variation and your dog's physicality will change as he or she gets older. The goal of each massage session is relaxation. It's beneficial for both you and your dog.

This is a graduation level. You will see that your dog will become more receptive to the variety of strokes that you are offering and the session will have become longer.

To begin the Advanced Sequence, print a list of the thirteen steps on a piece of paper and place it next to you on the mat.

Methodically go through the strokes, starting from the jaw moving through the body to the tail and see how your dog relaxes into each one.

By this time, you will intuitively know how long to stay in each area and how much your dog likes or doesn't like a stroke. Everything is flexible and relaxed. The joy of seeing your dog in a happy state of well-being while feeling balanced and relaxed yourself is an accomplishment. You and your dog have mastered the basic strokes of massage. Congratulations to both you and your happy dog!

The Advanced Massage Sequence from Head to Tail

1. Jaw: petrissage

2. Crown: petrissage or effleurage

3. Ears: effleurage

4. Neck: petrissage or web petrissage

5. Shoulders: compression or petrissage

6. Arms: squeezing compression and web petrissage

7. Legs: squeezing compression

8. Back: effleurage

9. Ribs: fingertip effleurage

10. Gluteus muscles: compression or effleurage

11. Thighs: variety

12. Tail: squeezing compression

13. Finish: brush off

Massage in an Emergency

Here is a scenario where a dog owner used a massage technique on his black Labrador during an emergency:

> *"I'd been learning the massage sequences when recently my dog started whimpering in pain. He got his front feet onto the bed, but couldn't get any further. His right back leg was not extended. I found a very hard lump just in front of the top leg muscle. I used the petrissage massage techniques down his side and along his leg. Within a few minutes, the knot in the muscle was gone. He must have had a charlie horse or the equivalent. It took fifteen minutes for the heavy breathing to stop; he was scared. He walked it off for a few minutes and then laid down to nap."*

Dog Massage for Children

One of the problems with dogs in households with small children is that oftentimes a child's only involvement with a dog is with play and rough-housing. From the dog's perspective, the child becomes another play object, like a large chew toy. Children can be knocked down, scratched, or bitten by a dog that is just exhibiting normal play behavior. Children are often encouraged to play with their dog, bringing both child and dog into a very excitable state. By introducing a child to canine massage, one can change the dog's perspective and its relationship with the child. It will also teach the child to respect that their dog is a sensitive, living being. Effleurage and compression are especially easy for a child to learn, as seen in the DVD demonstration between Rags and Ariana.

Teaching a child to be gentle with an animal is a gift of a lifetime. It will give the child the confidence that he or she has learned a skill that is positive for the behavior of the family pet.

Massage Works Wonders

Dogs communicate on an energetic level and massage is a direct path to their life's energy. It increases the flow of energy as a stimulation for the brain and increases circulation and motion. Massage can also decrease the discomfort of arthritis, overworked muscle tissue, and reactions to medications. It's not just about pain. Massage is preventative. In younger dogs it helps prevent injury and maintains balance. Life spans for senior dogs may be extended through massage.

The benefits of massage are not only good for your dog but serve as an education about the full health of your pet every time you partner in a massage session. Massage is the awakening for a dog owner to learn what is possible for his or her dog. Your dog will move better, sleep differently, and have increased range of motion like the instinctive wild animal he or she really is.

CHAPTER FOUR

Beyond the Bark

Imagine that you're walking your dog on-leash down the road. Your dog perks up upon seeing another person and dog coming your way. Your dog starts barking. The other person's dog starts barking.

You say to yourself, "Okay now, everyone be friendly," but your gut instinct and your ears are telling you something else.

The approaching dog's bark is intense, pronounced deeply from its chest. The dog pulls its owner closer to your dog. What do you do? You have a choice. You could let the dogs meet and smell each other as dogs do and then see if they become friendly or aggressive toward each other. You could also keep your dog pulled to the side and away from the approaching dog. Whatever your decision, your instincts are a valuable skill. You *heard* the other dog escalating the intensity of its barks and you *saw* that your dog was becoming submissive in his or her body language. As dog owners, we have a responsibility to protect our dog by sensing— along with our dog—if these encounters are going to be nice or not. Just as in our human world, we don't assume everyone we meet is going to be friendly just because they come into our path on the street. The criteria of age, breed, gender, behavioral training, and attitude of the dog owner all come into play when dogs meet. This common scenario illustrates how important your awareness is. Hearing the pitches, tones, intensity, expression, and phrasing of the language of your dog is an excellent way to evaluate many aspects of our dog's daily life.

As dog owners we learn to be sensitive to our dog's vocalization, whether we are aware of it or not. Our dogs have trained us to respond. Along with their body posturing, they bark and express subtle sounds to tell us when they need to go out; when they want food, our attention, play time; or when they have accidentally locked themselves behind a door. The faintest vocalization and we are up from our chair to get our dog's leash or go into action to fix dinner. If you listen to how your dog vocalizes, you will be amazed at the vast range of sounds. Most dogs have about a four-octave range, or forty-eight note-like sounds. When you listen to the *Relaxation Music for Dogs* CD, you will notice that I do not use human speaking or human singing in the music. Words have limited meaning for dogs and require interpretation of story through analytical thinking. Using words does not add to the calming effect for dogs. Rather, the journey of the instrumental music is soothing for them. In my research studies, I learned that dogs prefer long, meditative tones and lilting melodies. I want your dog to relax with this music and if I had added a human voice to each piece, it would cause your dog to perk up and be alert.

The variety of expression in your dog's vocal language becomes more apparent as you listen to your dog's subtle nuances of communication. Some breeds are more vocal than others, and there is variety even within a breed.

In 1984, renowned acoustic biologist Katy Payne, along with other field researchers, discovered that elephants communicate with each other using infrasonic sounds. (Infrasonic sounds are frequencies that exist below the human hearing range.) By uncovering animal language, we continue to broaden our human view of the intricacies and complexities of other species. Careful listening and learning of your dog's vocalizations will open your awareness to the amazing repertoire of canine language.

Dogs have both open and closed muzzle vocalizations. Each group ranges in sounds from low to high pitches and soft to loud volumes. Barking is just one of many sounds that make up the musical language of a dog. I say "musical" because all the elements of music are part of their language. There are long and short phrases; dynamic volumes, tones, and rhythmic patterns; and emotional expression.

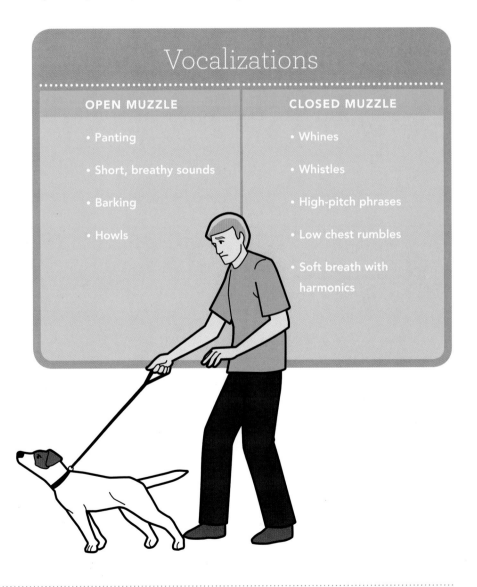

Vocalizations

OPEN MUZZLE	CLOSED MUZZLE
• Panting	• Whines
• Short, breathy sounds	• Whistles
• Barking	• High-pitch phrases
• Howls	• Low chest rumbles
	• Soft breath with harmonics

Variations on the Theme of Bark

How many variations of barks does your dog have? Does your dog have different barks for different people, animals, and things? You might want to take some time to count how many types of barks your dog actually expresses over a few days. Dog barks can explode as an intense first sound and die down into a sequence of pants. Some dog barks are short and consistent of pitch. Others have a rhythm to them, with an equal interval of time spaced between each utterance. There are barks that start off high in pitch and then go down into the chest before returning to the high pitch. There are combinations of barks that have longer phrases, especially when your dog is excited, with breathy panting starting the sequence.

Variations on the Theme of Whine

This requires a little more intense listening on your part. Dogs use their more subtle vocalizations in a vast range of whines for a variety of reasons. These whines range from low sounds to almost imperceptibly high pitches. Being in a quiet environment makes it easier to hear them. Your dog's subtle communications go beyond whining for a treat. The breathy high frequency whines or utterances are part of the whole language. Some of these whines can be so high, they create harmonics in the dog's muzzle. If I converse with Rags with a few minutes of imitating his pitches and phrases of whines, I can sometimes hear a very quiet, throaty breath with a high harmonic. Dogs are quite the virtuosos! The beautiful aspect of these subtle utterances is that our dogs seem to share their most soft vocalizations with their owners while using their louder barks to communicate to the outside world. There is certainly much more to learn about the language of our dogs as we live with them from day to day.

Responding to the Bark

Understanding your dog's vocal language will help you keep him or her calm.

Understanding your dog's vocal language will help you keep him or her calm. If you are indifferent to your dog's bark, he or she will continue and escalate the pitch until you acknowledge the communication in some way. Don't let barking get out of hand. It's stressful for you and your dog. Responding to the bark is part of controlling your dog's behavior and maintaining a calm environment. Barking alerts us to various things: there is another dog outside, a thunderstorm is approaching, there is a truck rumbling, there is someone at the door. Dogs do not bark for no reason. Alternately, if we are responsive to barking and subtle communications, our dog gains the confidence of knowing its place. That is good companionship.

Talking in "Sixth Sense"

We have so many sounds, beeps, and buzzes from technology and appliances in our homes, we may not realize that our dogs are often engaged in looking at us with a silent stare. This is their "sixth sense" communication. Have you ever felt the focused energy of your dog as he sits next to you, piercing your space with this silent tap on the shoulder of, "Hi. I'm here. I need something."? The quiet calm of dog communication may be their way of asking us to develop *our* sixth sense to better communicate with them.

Conversations with Your Dog

We ask our dog to learn the inflection of our words and the meanings of these words to respond to us in a specific way. Adding a little dog language to the mix can create a fun conversation. Have you ever barked along with your dog, or matched your dog's vocalizations? Mimicking smaller utterances can become a lengthy dialogue. Going back and forth in different utterances is an experiment that your dog will respond to happily. Dogs love you as their human family and conversing with your dog in its own language can be an interesting and creative interaction for any dog owner.

When Dogs Lose Their Hearing

When your dog loses its hearing, vibrations that can be felt through the paws and body become more important. Hearing-impaired dogs have increased sensitivity to strong vibrations from trucks on the road outside or appliances in your home. This change may cause stress and anxiety. You can still play the *Relaxation Music for Dogs* CD since your pet will now respond to vibrations emanating from your stereo speakers.

In addition, communicating with your dog through touch will become more important. Your dog will look to your body language for visual cues. Set aside time for more frequent massage sessions to help relieve the stress as your dog shifts his or her dependency to senses other than hearing.

Communication Is Key

For many reasons, it has been the curiosity of mankind to train living creatures to imitate human behavior through sound and movement. In recent years, researchers have uncovered the depths and complexities of animal communication. This research has shown not only the ability of the vast range of communication of animals but the *need* to express states of emotion through language. With digital technologies, we have already learned of the complex communications and language of dolphins, whales, and elephants. As we progress in these wonderful discoveries, we are diminishing our dominance over animals. Instead, we are uncovering more similarities of family structure and communication. We know, as dog owners, that our dogs teach us about companionship and show us the gift of unconditional love. Work to understand canine language a little more and go beyond the bark.

CHAPTER FIVE

Rhythms, Walks & Companionship

One of the most pleasurable and healthy parts of living with our dogs is the partnership of walking. Going for a walk with your dog may feel like a necessary daily activity but it is much, much more.

Walking with your dog is one of the most beautiful and valuable parts of your relationship because it is a time that balances communication and partnership. A walk activates both human *and* dog senses: breathing the outdoor air together, living life in the present, and exercising.

There is an abundance of expert advice for dog owners learning to train puppies and adult dogs. Walking our dog in a controlled state of behavior is one of the most important aspects of training. If a dog's lifespan is an average of fifteen years and you walk your dog at least two times a day, that's approximately 10,950 times that you will be taking your dog out for a walk. That's a lot of walks! Making your walks interesting over all this time is a creative challenge and creates a more meaningful relationship through these shared experiences.

Dogs look forward to these moments. The road, the street, or the trail is where your dog enjoys your company while happily activating the senses. If we stop to think about the significance of walking with our dogs, regardless of their breed and age, it's inter-species exercise at its best.

It's important to note that we walk with our thoughts and dogs walk with their noses. A harmony occurs in this way, as our dog helps us to get out of our inner monologue. In time though, I believe we eventually bend to natural instincts and join them in the journey.

You know you have reached the "way of the dog" when together you both:

- **perk up at the same sound**

- **catch a whiff of the same smell**

- **stop to look at the same interesting spot**

- **react to a movement in the distance**

Our dogs are completely willing to make this a give-and-take journey. Dog owners usually start the pace of a walk until our dog finds something absolutely necessary to sniff or analyze . . . like a previously made paw print in the snow or a garbage can marked by other cool city dogs. Taking "the walk" is an agreement between you and your dog, and what companionship is all about.

Remember in my introduction I expressed the commonality between musicians and dogs? Taking a walk with your dog is like a musical composition. Walking together has phrasing, tempos, dynamics, and form.

The Composition of a Walk

Phrasing—Phrasing has a beginning, a high point, and an end. Walks have their own phrasing and there is always one interesting point in the middle, even if it is as simple as a trip to pick up the mail down the road.

Tempo—Tempo is the pace at which you and your dog walk. Some days are energetic and some days require a slower pace. Whatever your pace, your dog is aware of your energy level and adjusts to your tempo. You are true partners.

Dynamics—There are dynamics (soft and loud) to every part of the day. There is always an interesting dynamic to experience along the way: a walk through a noisy construction zone or a pause in the park to enjoy a treat.

Form—Walking full circle. In Native American folklore, it is said to complete a journey you must always make a circle. Any walking route for a dog is an adventure. Instead of returning the same way you came, find a different route home to complete the circle of the journey.

I know, as a dog owner myself, that there are times when bending to your dog's demand to go outside isn't the first preference of activity. . . especially when it's freezing out, there are wind gusts, or it's the hottest part of the day. But the best walks are when we are equally enthusiastic to go outside, get some fresh air, and be with our walking partner. The benefits are all positive. The exercise is good for your heart, the outdoors stimulates the senses, and walking is a form of relaxation that diminishes stress.

Varying Your Walk Repertoire

There are many methods to teach puppies how to learn to walk on-leash. During your walk-training time, make sure that you use your voice all along the way. Your dog is imprinting the inflection of your voice to learn and understand your commands. Keep your voice in a high, clear pitch, because that is the range of hearing that is best for them. For puppy training, pay attention to your intention with clear inflection!

LEASH COMMUNICATION

Your dog's leash is literally its connection to you. The tether or leash is very similar to the reins a rider uses with his horse. Every subtle motion of the hand means something to your dog and provides instructions. When your dog is in physical balance with you and is aware of your intentions, walking on-leash can be an exercise in good communication as well as an enjoyable physical experience. Yanking at a leash and yelling won't teach a dog anything. On the contrary, it is the most subtle of commands, physical posturing, and your voice that engages a dog's full willingness to please and learn. You can practice these subtleties of command in different ways, especially through walking in partnership.

You know that your dog's way of walking is through its nose, eyes, and ears. Use the leash the way a conductor would use a baton to lead an orchestra and adjust the leash to keep your dog engaged and aware of your directions. Establish a rhythm to your walk and keep your dog at that pace.

ON-LEASH WALKING TECHNIQUES

Here are a few tips to introduce variety during your on-leash walks.

- As a simple training exercise, count a certain number of steps in a pattern and then stop to request a sit/stay. Repeat the counting pattern for your dog to adhere to and then release into freeform walking. Then back to pattern walking. Always train to your dog's stamina and abilities.

- Try cardio walking by bumping up the pace to a brisk walk or a run. Great for you, great for your dog. Vary the tempo so your dog remains alert and watches you for new commands.

- Without speaking your command, see how gentle you can be with the leash until your dog sits or stops. Then, use another gentle tug on the leash to start the walk again. The more you train your dog, the more he or she will understand subtlety.

- You probably always hold the leash with the same hand when you walk your dog. Try switching hands in order to use different shoulder and arm muscles. Changing habitual use of body muscles keeps us aware and maintains physical balance.

The bond of walking with your dog off-leash is an exercise in *trust*. Your dog will enjoy the confidence and freedom of choosing a path while being with its "person." That is a happy state for a dog! The outdoor air will carry the frequency of your voice, no matter how far your dog wanders. Practice bringing your dog back to your side with a vocal command. At first, don't let your dog go too far. He or she wants to know that you are near. If your dog is concentrating on a scent, it may take a little more coaxing to get him or her out of this gear. You can rely upon your dog's acute hearing to acknowledge your presence. If this is the beginning of your dog's off-leash experience, use treats to keep him or her engaged. Your dog won't travel far knowing you have a favorite treat in your pocket.

This freedom of movement is the best time to run, chase, and play catch. This is an interaction that makes for a good dog day. You will see it in the calm your dog feels when he or she returns home, goes to a special spot to lay down, and exhales a deep sigh. Making time in your schedule for off-leash partnership walks with your dog will create joyful memories to look back on.

OBSERVING WALKS

The more years we live with a dog, walking in partnership develops into new pleasures and dimensions of experience. Do you find yourself talking to your dog? Do you notice the little things because your dog has taught you to observe nature? Dogs clearly teach us to observe the path along the way. It is one of their greatest gifts to us as dog owners.

LISTENING WALKS

Our dog's hearing sensitivity while walking helps us train our own ears to hear better. Practice hearing where the sound is coming from that your dog is pausing to hear. Listening for faint or distant sounds can enhance a person's hearing abilities. When we walk alongside our dogs, they are not only sniffing and seeing where they are going but they are also hearing our footsteps. Tune in to hearing your own footsteps and then walk a little faster and watch your dog pick up the pace.

WALKING WITH FRIENDS

Make time to walk with friends and their dogs. Dogs need the balance of being with their own species. Being in the state of "dog" for them entails exercising their instincts. It is a joy to see our dogs in motion. Seeing your dog play with another dog is so much fun!

Emotional Companionship

The affection of a dog is a most precious gift! You come home from work or school, it was a long day, and your dog is ecstatic to see you. You sit down and your dog sits next to you. Your eyes catch your dog's eyes. Our dog seems to say, "Are you ok? Should we go for a walk? Shall we play?" This loving face melts away the stresses of the day!

Curiously, many cultures around the world do not accept the notion that animals are emotional beings. However, we know—just by living with our dogs so intimately—that they express empathy, love, and caring. They show sadness, like remaining by the door when a family member leaves. Dogs feel the loss when a family member or pet-mate passes away. Dogs show the pleasure of being massaged, as you can vividly see in the DVD accompanying this kit.

A dog's companionship is about more than just loyalty. Your dog is in full partnership with you. He or she knows when you are stressed and knows your states of joy. Dogs particularly love our joys because happy energy is their favorite state of being. When your emotions are lively, your dog reacts by wagging his or her tail. Dogs partner with us in emotional companionship every day. This flow of emotions is a treasured part of living with dogs.

CHAPTER SIX

Common Canine
Problems & Solutions

We've come a long way in our society from the days when dogs were chained to a doghouse and "dog care" meant a plate of meat scraps and a bowl of water. Today, dogs are accepted as important members of the family, participating in virtually every aspect of their owners' lives.

The high regard for "the dog" in contemporary western culture is evident in advertising, in the proliferation of pet store chains, and in the thousands of different services now available for dog care. Imagine explaining the concept of doggie spas to someone living in the early 1900s!

There are still some aspects of a modern dog's life, though, that need to be improved. These areas of concern can be very subtle, but they have a strong impact on canine well-being. It is the responsibility of dog owners to be aware of these subtleties and to help their dog live more comfortably in the human world.

As members of our home, our dogs have many ways of letting us know when things are just not right. In addition to physical symptoms and injuries that should be resolved by veterinarian care, there are other signs of common canine problems that should become part of every dog owner's awareness.

Careful observation of our dogs on a daily "check up" basis is our responsibility. It doesn't take much. Making sure that they are eating and drinking normally and observing their daily eliminations is essential. But we can often tell if something is wrong just by looking at our dog's body language and energy level. Always trust your instincts about your animal's well-being. How they behave on the outside tells us what is happening on the inside.

The following are common problems that can result in negative behaviors and physical distress. All can be resolved with a little effort on your part, creating amazing and magical opportunities to enrich your dog's life in your home and strengthen your human-doggie relationship.

Every Dog Needs a Job

Dogs need jobs? Yes! Your dog's aimlessness is often a root cause of negative canine behavior. Dogs need a purpose, whether it is protecting the house; making sure the family members are all present and accounted for; or digging, hunting, or alerting us to sounds, strangers, and smells. When a dog knows its job, he or she will commit to it until the last breath. Think of all the different breeds of hunting dogs, herding dogs, rodent catchers, and guard dogs. Their breeding prepared them for specific jobs long before we brought them into our homes as pets and family members. Though we love them and take care of them, dogs without jobs become bored, lazy, and inactive if they are not engaged in pursuing their life's purpose. Appealing to the natural breed instincts of your dog through games, indoor toys, and outdoor play is a way to exercise these deep instincts. Problems arise when nervous energy and anxiety accumulate because we impose limits on our dog's instincts.

If your dog is a mixed breed, try to determine which breed behavior is its dominant tendency. Make it a part of your dog's day to chase, catch a ball, hunt, herd, or play sniff-and-find. Once you have acknowledged your dog's job, reinforce its "working" behavior with praise, treats, a pat with "good job," or a favorite spot for massage! (And, of course, plenty of kisses and hugs!) Dogs know when they have satisfied you, and this makes them happy.

My wonderful dog Rags is a terrier mix—part Lhaso Apso and part Wheaton terrier. His purpose is to alert us to approaching strangers and his breeding behavior is "to hunt and herd." I reinforce with "good job" praise when he barks to alert me that there is a car or person approaching our house. I thank him for protecting us. When my husband and I take walks in the woods with Rags off-leash, we play "hunt and seek" behind the trees. I say enthusiastically to Rags, "Go find Alan!" Nose glued to the ground, Rags starts his detective work. He goes into high sensing alert and soon Alan is found! Treats and praise follow. This is a game that stimulates Rags' instincts and makes for a good dog day.

Create your own games to tap into your dog's breed behaviors, and praise your dog for just being the dog he or she is supposed to be!

> *Dogs need a purpose, whether it is protecting the house; making sure the family members are all present and accounted for; or digging, hunting, or alerting us to sounds, strangers, and smells.*

Harmony with Children

Children and dogs have a very similar life force. They are both agile in their movements and have hearing abilities superior to human adults. When we are born and throughout childhood, our human hearing sensitivities are acute. Unfortunately, they diminish as we get older. This commonality between dogs and children can affect their relationship. Toddlers and children in general often frighten dogs because of high-pitched voices that frequently reach the ultra-high agitating level of dog hearing. But cultivating the relationship between children and dogs can become an area of learning that can enrich their lives together. Teaching children to be kind and gentle to an animal can have a positive influence that lasts a lifetime.

There are several areas where problems can develop inside and outside the home and each scenario can have solutions and positive results for dog and dog owner.

YOUR DOG AND THE NEW BABY

The new baby is coming and your dog has always been the well-established focus of attention in the family. Many couples are concerned when they anticipate the birth of their baby. "How will my dog react and behave around the baby?" "How will the scent and sounds of the baby affect our beloved dog?" A new baby is an adjustment for people and dogs alike. To smooth the transition, consider your dog's need for your attention as a scheduled part of your day. While you are with your baby, play the *Relaxation Music for Dogs* CD for your dog to keep the atmosphere calm. The music will mask some of the commotion around the baby and the sounds of the newborn. An added benefit of the music is that it is designed for the comfort of high frequency hearing sensitivities and therefore can be used effectively for calming the baby as well.

Make sure a member of your family gives your dog full attention each day with a long walk outdoors or a toss of a toy. Dogs' instincts for family are so similar to ours that in a short time your dog will instinctively understand the new home life scenario.

TODDLERS AND DOGS

The size and vocal pitch of a toddler can be a threatening or scary experience for your dog. Make sure that you don't leave these two alone to work it out! An authoritative voice is required—for both toddler and dog—to calm any unexpected aggressive behaviors. Toddlers can innocently grip or pull on a dog's body in a way that can cause a dog to react with a growl, nip, or bite. Defining the relationship between your dog and toddler can be a wonderful opportunity to teach your child how to be gentle and kind to another living creature. It's a valuable life lesson.

Teach your child:

- the massage techniques on the DVD

- that soft and gentle tones of music are soothing for dogs

- not to go face to face with an unknown dog

- to always ask a dog owner if it's okay to pet a dog

- that animals are to be respected as living, feeling beings

YOUR DOG MEETING CHILDREN ON THE STREET

Think about how your dog perks up as he or she approaches another person on the street. Your dog is ready to either protect you or make a new friend. If your dog is off-leash, make sure that he or she is always in earshot of your vocal commands. If on-leash, bring your dog a little closer to you to indicate that you are in control of the approaching situation.

Many people, children and adults, don't really know how to approach a dog for a safe and friendly encounter. Though their intentions are kind and friendly, bending down to go face to face with a dog can be a signal of aggression, one that can cause your dog to snap or bite. Meeting a child on the street is a great opportunity for you to show him or her how to safely greet and pet dogs. The child may ask, "May I pet your dog?" Then explain that it's good to offer the dog a closed hand in front of the dog's nose. If the dog shows that it is willing to be petted, then explain that it is best to start petting a dog from the top of the head towards the tail while talking softly. Monitor how your dog is reacting to the child. If your dog is balanced and responsive to your commands, this will be a positive training session for your dog as well.

Sometimes, such a simple moment will have a lifelong influence on a child's positive connection to animals. Many adults fear dogs and that mistrust often stems from negative childhood-animal experiences. Some adults who have had a single bad experience with a dog will say as a blanket statement, "I don't like dogs." At any age, we can overcome our fear of animals.

The Home Stereo and Your Dog

For dogs, low frequencies such as loud drums can easily generate stress and the "get ready to flee" response. To a dog, very low or very high frequency information and resonant vibrations are sounds that are indistinguishable from a loud vehicle or thunder. This uncertainty, combined with the fact that they cannot locate the source of these vibrations, causes them to react with their defense instincts. If a dog is sitting by a speaker on the floor and the bass frequencies go below 60 cycles per second or 60Hz, the sound exerts pressure on the dog's middle and inner ear, which could be painful. The sound coming from the speaker manipulates the air, pushing it at a volume and frequency at the low edge of the hearing range of the dog. This may subtly cause discomfort and an irate behavioral reaction. If subwoofer speakers sit on bare floors in your home, your dog may be especially agitated as vibrations are felt through his or her paws making contact with the floor. To solve this problem, place a carpet under the speakers. (To understand how your pet feels such pressure, place your hand on the sound source of a radio or TV and you will feel the pressure of the sound against your hand.)

Outside Noise

Outside noise has a huge impact on canine behavior. Your dog hears and reacts to the sirens of fire trucks and police cars, the rumble of trucks on the highway, or the roar of a motorcycle. All of this has an impact on your dog's health and behavior. Acknowledging that we can't live somewhere simply to accommodate our dog's hearing sensitivities, we can find ways to make our dog more comfortable with intense noise.

Keep your dog's nesting spot or crate padded to absorb some of the low vibrations. Place a CD player by your dog's resting area and play the *Relaxation Music for Dogs* CD on repeat mode throughout the day to help mask some of the outside noise levels. Use the massage techniques illustrated in Chapter 3 and on the DVD included in this kit to help release the physical tensions your dog internalizes as a result of low and high frequency vibrations assaulting his or her body. This may seem like an excessive level of care, but I have consulted with dog owners across the country whose dogs have constant anxiety because of thunderstorm noise or truck rumbles. It is a small sacrifice of our time and energy to make our dog as comfortable as possible.

Breeding and Birthing

People involved with breeding dogs look for ways to provide as much comfort as possible to the mother during this delicate process. The use of music during birthing is a good way to provide the canine mom with a calm, soothing environment. Many people who breed dogs (and other animals) use music to diminish distress during labor. The music is also a way of masking other noises in the environment that might increase the anxiety of the mother.

Doggie Day Care and Spas

Lucky dogs! While we're at work, they are having a day of fun! Our pets deserve it, though.

Some dogs exhibit shaking and other anxious behaviors when going into a new environment with other dogs. Staff members of day care centers are experts at welcoming and escorting your dog into this environment, but you can aid the process with a brief massage sequence and a treat. Then hand your dog over to the staff person along with some treats-to-go—and you know your dog will follow wherever that bag is going! If the doggie day care provider or spa can play the relaxation music where your dog is kept, the music will be an association of "home." It is a good idea to have the CD travel with your dog. Whether at day care, the spa, the groomer, or with a pet sitter, your dog will associate the music with feeling comfortable and relaxed, even in new surroundings. If you are traveling with your dog to a pet-friendly hotel, play the *Relaxation Music for Dogs* CD whenever you leave the room. This can help your dog calm down and keep him or her from barking as a result of separation anxiety.

Age and Loss of Some Senses

Clearly, dogs are living longer today because of better dog owner and veterinary care. We also see more mixed breeding of dog species, which enhances life span but also complicates common physical expectancies. Therefore, understanding your elderly dog and how to manage this stage of his or her life is a relatively new area of learning for a dog owner. With common

If your dog's sight seems to be failing, and going up and down stairs becomes a problem, you can help by using aroma therapy scents along the stair path. Your dog will easily follow the scent.

physical symptoms such as arthritis, loss of hearing, and muscular-skeletal imbalances, managing an older dog having trouble with normal activities becomes an important focus. Using the massage techniques learned in this book will aid stiffness in joints and help to increase circulation for easier body movement in your middle aged and elderly dog. Many dogs lose their hearing as they get older, and using music for relaxation becomes a moot point. However, regular massage sessions can help your dog activate his or her other senses. Stimulation of the skin can aid circulation and muscular-skeletal conditions. Your touch becomes more important to communicate safety and reassurance.

Elderly dogs can also lose their sense of sight. If your dog's sight seems to be failing, and going up and down stairs becomes a problem, you can help by using aroma therapy scents along the stair path. Your dog will easily follow the scent. Though dogs will eventually adjust to any disability by depending more heavily on other senses, massage can help your dog maintain confidence and comfort in this phase of his or her life.

Lunging

One of the most common ways dogs get themselves killed is by running out into the road and being hit by a car. This behavior comes from their instinct to protect their territory and attack the threat.

If your dog has a habit of lunging towards trucks and other vehicles while on a walk, you can adjust the behavior over time. First, try to hear what your dog is hearing when you are on the street. This is a good sensory exercise to heighten your own hearing and awareness. Keep your dog close to you on a shortened leash as you see or hear a jogger, car, or other vehicle approaching. You can teach your dog to not lunge at vehicles with a tight leash and a "no" reprimand. Then, as the vehicle passes, give words of praise. Continue to anticipate approaching vehicles and keep a

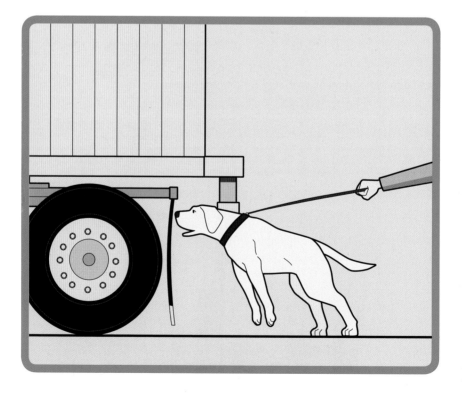

tight leash and a reprimand at the ready, with praise afterwards. In time, a quick, gentle tug on the leash will be the signal that will prevent your dog from lunging. Eventually your dog will become more interested in continuing to explore the rich sensory world around him or her than reacting to vehicles.

Hospitalization and Recuperation

Any post-surgery period is a physically tenuous time for a dog. The disorientation of awakening from anesthesia is highly distressing. An atmosphere of music can provide comfort and mask some of the beeps and sounds of medical equipment that can aggravate hearing sensitivity. The *Relaxation Music for Dogs* CD is played at many veterinary hospitals around the country and continues to be of benefit to animals during this potentially traumatic time.

Surgery and Illness

Rest, calm, and quiet are elements your dog needs in order to heal. It is a vulnerable time for your dog, as it is hard for him or her to put aside natural impetuses to engage all of the senses.

The music in this kit is composed with meditative phrases and long tones, which dogs like. The consistent non-jarring volume throughout will also help your dog rest. Soothing music affects dogs on a cellular level—they will respond to the sounds by releasing muscle tensions. Play the *Relaxation Music for Dogs* CD as a soothing accompaniment to familiar household sounds during this time when massage and the usual belly rubs will have to wait until your dog is feeling better.

Adopting a Shelter Dog

You've already solved the biggest problem in this scenario: you've
opened your heart and welcomed a dog in need into your home. That is
already a great gift. Nevertheless, your new dog's nervousness, stemming
from transition, and his or her reaction to unfamiliar surroundings needs
to be carefully addressed. I must give dogs credit as a species, though,
as their sixth sense of "this is going to be good and safe" is a display of
amazing perception. They just know that you are going to take care of

them. But your new dog may also be in survival mode and easing him or her into an environment of trust can be a challenge. There is a wide range of transitional behaviors that dogs display when joining a new pack. To help a new dog adjust to your home, consider how dogs perceive the world and interact accordingly.

HEARING

Don't play loud—potentially agitating—music during your dog's introduction to his or her new home. Create a calm atmosphere. Let the dog explore this new environment. Let him or her learn the tone of your pack-leader voice. Make sure the environment is welcoming. With the cooperation of everyone in your home, introduce the dog to each member of the family. However, let your dog know that *you* are the leader and that *you* will be the person to look to for behavioral cues.

SMELL

Your dog will use his or her nose to thoroughly explore and evaluate your home. Even if you close some doors to restrict access for the time being, letting him or her roam will provide a sense of security and prove that the corners and open spaces of your home are safe.

TASTE

Set up a space that says to your dog, "this is where you will find your food." Eating is such a strong survival instinct that knowing he or she can have a bowl of food to eat right then and there will pretty much have your dog sign-on-the-dotted-line ready to stay in your home forever!

TOUCH

Touch brings calm and trust to your new dog. Prepare your dog's bed
pad or crate ahead of his or her arrival, and dedicate a special doggie
downtime space. Your dog's nesting pad will tell him or her that this
is home. Your dog may be quite exhausted from the emotion of living
at and leaving the shelter. If your dog is receptive, use a few massage
techniques learned from the accompanying DVD to create a bond
through touch. It will take a few weeks before you can truly evaluate
your dog's actual physical state, sensitivities, and favorite ways of being
touched. Be patient with this process.

Bring your dog to each room in your home that you will allow your dog to access. Talk along the way and he or she will begin to key in to your vocal pitch to learn what you do and don't want. As your dog learns the layout of your home, you can gently try some training words to figure out which, if any, commands he or she knows. Your new dog will also see that you are calm and in command—a position he or she will respond to while learning about you as the family leader.

INTRODUCING A DOG TO YOUR CAT

If possible, bring something of your cat's, like a toy, with you to the shelter. Let the dog smell the toy to learn your cat's smell. When your dog sees and smells your cat in your home, your dog will associate the smell and this will help the transition. Most often, dogs and cats can work out their territories and relationships by themselves without excessive human intervention.

Talkers and Barkers

In the home, dogs bark and talk to us. They are trying to get our attention and tell us something important. Barking can become a crescendo of pitch and intense energy in our household. We may start yelling back to attempt to quiet things down, creating a cycle of more barking and more yelling with increasing intensity. Try to have the discipline to stand quietly before your dog as he or she barks and you will discover that he or she will calm down as *you* calm down. Dogs pick up so many of their behavioral cues from us that we can assist them by exhibiting the behavior we're requesting. Even if your dog continues to bark, remain calm and try to discover what he or she is telling you. Does he hear something? Is she alerting you to some noise outside? With some effort, you can control your dog's barking.

Memory in Dogs

Our pet's memory, through emotional and sensory associations, is a meaningful aspect of their life experience. There is a very clear example of canine memory in my own life with my dog Rags. One day while at home, the batteries to our smoke detector failed and triggered an extremely high-pitched sound throughout the house. I frantically tried to install a new battery as quickly as I could because not only was it piercing to my ears, but I saw that Rags was in an extreme state of shivering, tail tucked under, and shaking—unable to escape the sound. It was only after an hour of holding him that he calmed down and relaxed his body into a normal state of calm. A few weeks later, I observed an interesting repeat of this scenario. While in our backyard, a red-winged blackbird came up to the bird feeder and emitted a series of quick high pitches. Within an instant, Rags began to shake vigorously with his tail tucked under. I realized that this was the same pitch and piercing sound as the smoke detector. To Rags' canine interpretation, this meant a repeat of "whatever that horrible sound is, I am scared and this could mean danger." I began to hold him to calm him and brought him indoors. The recognition of the pitch of the smoke detector and the high frequency of the blackbird were similar enough for Rags to trigger his aural memory. To diminish this memory, since the blackbird was going to enjoy our birdseed more often than not, I spent time with him outdoors going through some massage touches and verbal assurances as soon as I saw the blackbird had returned to the feeder. Now, when the blackbird utters its first chirp, Rags raises his head from his nap and gives me a worried look and I assure him that it's okay. As stressful experiences for your dog become apparent to you, you may want to keep a journal to log in these scenarios ... especially if they are physically or aurally traumatic. In looking over your notes, you may discover patterns or roots of behavior that need to be addressed.

Chemicals and Floors

Dogs live on a level that we rarely experience in our daily lives—floor level, that is. Dogs lie on our floors, they roll around on the ground, and they pick up treats from our floors. This can be a problem if we use chemicals on our floors or have carpets that have been chemically treated. As you analyze your dog's behavior, stop to think whether you have used a new cleaning chemical on your floor that synchronizes with the timing of your dog becoming ill. We don't know for sure, but we can guess that with our dog's acute sense of smell, floor cleaners may be directly related to symptoms displayed.

Salts and Sand on Roads

If you live in an area where salt and sand combinations are used for travel on snow and ice, it is a good idea to have a towel handy to wash or rub off salt from the paws and mouth of your dog. Salt is a known skin irritant, especially if it becomes imbedded in your dog's paws or is swallowed.

Giving Back to Your Dog

With your *Zen Dog* kit, you are now empowered with massage skills and the knowledge to use music for the well-being of your dog. Anytime you want to change the environment to elicit a sense of calm for your dog, play the CD and watch your dog settle down and relax. Anytime you and your dog want to use a massage session for relaxing, you can do so with confidence. The two of you will surely find new and creative ways to dovetail the music and massage techniques with your own personal lifestyle.

We all love our dogs. Our dog's unconditional love for us is a joy. The gift of music and the loving touch of massage are now in your hands for your dog's wellness for a stress-free, happy, and healthy life.

About the Author

An expert in the field of pet relaxation, Janet Marlow, M.A., has appeared frequently on Animal Planet and is the creator of a music CD series for dogs, cats, and horses. She's a well-known lecturer, composer, and member of the Animal Behavior Society and the Connecticut Horse Council. She is also a consultant for New York Presbyterian Dog Therapy Program.

In addition to her work in the animal field, Ms. Marlow has a distinguished career as a recording artist on the ten-string guitar, and as a composer for film and television. She's combined twenty years of experience as a professional musician with her research on the hearing sensitivities and interpretive capacities of dogs to create acoustic environments conducive to canine well-being.

Acknowledgments

My appreciation to the following people for their support and encouragement to go beyond the music: Alan, Colin, and Ross Brennan; Dana and Mel Toomey and Shalom; Nancy Stokes; Pamela Holick; LaMyra Haynes; Patti Moran; Susan Begasse; Margaret Hurst; Wendy Broeder; Hedda Von Goeben; Dr. Laura Carey; Dr. Mary G. Battista; Dr. Dale V. Atkins; Steve Tankanow; Teresa Gagnon; Alison Starkey; Pat, Vicki, and Julia Daly; Stephen Rekas; and Susan Hannah. My special thanks to Taylor Johnson of T.H.E. Audio for his master teaching in acoustic science; to Henry E. Heffner and Rickye S. Heffner for their research on auditory perceptions of animals; to my agent, Teresa Focarile, with gratitude for making this book and kit happen; to my editor, Andrea Rotondo, who understood the importance of this information and awareness for dog owners; and deep appreciation to my friends, Mary Pope Osborne and Will Osborne, for their light and love.